*Stepping Out
with Scott and Zelda*

Nostalgia or the flight of the heart: Montgomery as it was.

— F. Scott Fitzgerald, *The Note-Books*

Stepping Out with Scott and Zelda

Touring the Fitzgeralds' Montgomery

Máire Martello

NewSouth Books
Montgomery

NewSouth Books
105 S. Court Street
Montgomery, AL 36104

Publisher's Cataloging-in-Publication Data

Names: Martello, Máire, author.
Title: Stepping out with Scott and Zelda: touring the
Fitzgeralds' Montgomery / by Máire Martello.
Description: Montgomery : NewSouth Books, [2021].
Identifiers: 9781588384508 (trade paper) |
LCCN 2021947521
Subjects: Literary—Special interest—Travel. | East South
Central (AL, KY, MS, TN)—South—United States—
Travel. | 20th century—United States—History.

Design by Randall Williams

Printed in the United States of America

The Black Belt, defined by its dark, rich soil, stretches across central Alabama. It was the heart of the cotton belt. It was and is a place of great beauty, of extreme wealth and grinding poverty, of pain and joy. Here we take our stand, listening to the past, looking to the future.

Contents

Introduction

My journey to Montgomery began when my mother brought home two books from the library: Sheilah Graham's *Beloved Infidel* and Nancy Milford's *Zelda.* The beauty, talent and tragedy of Scott and Zelda Fitzgerald were catnip to a romantic teenager.

Thereafter, I spent much of my youth in Manhattan at the Palm Court attempting a gin fizz rickey or at the Biltmore Hotel waiting for a date under the lobby's famous clock. My walks along Nassau Street in Princeton called to mind not the current generation of young men but a breathlessly excited Fitzgerald dashing off to New York City to catch Ina Claire in *The Quaker Girl* or Hazel Dawn in *The Pink Lady.* When I made my first trip to Paris I didn't waste time at an outdoor café. I made my way to 14 rue de Tilsit to gaze up at the windows of the Fitzgeralds' rented apartment. I finagled my way into the Olympia Theater to see the dusty floors where Zelda spent so many fraught hours learning to dance with the Ballet Russe.

In 1997, when the F. Scott Fitzgerald Society announced a FitzFest in Montgomery, I pounced at the chance for a first visit. A rickety, unairconditioned bus took members to the Fitzgeralds' large rental home on

Felder Avenue, paused before the Elite Cafe where the couple had dined, and dropped us off at the Montgomery Museum of Fine Arts. There we were served pimento cheese hors d'oeuvres and shown Zelda's sinewy ballet figures and stunning paper dolls.

Striking out on my own that weekend, I found Zelda's grammar school in the Cottage Hill neighborhood and the remnants of her childhood home on Pleasant Avenue. It was on these grass-choked front steps where she was courted by Lieutenant F. Scott Fitzgerald in 1919. That evening my husband and I dined at the since-closed Sahara Restaurant on Norman Bridge Road. In a Southern city that justly prides itself on its civil rights victories, there was a moment of sharp dissonance when we were seated beneath a giant portrait of George Wallace.

In the fall of 2018, remembering this handsome city situated on a bend in the river, we bought a home in the leafy Cloverdale neighborhood. I was surprised to find that although local bookstores held tour guides to myriad historical sites, the Fitzgeralds' Montgomery was sadly neglected. It seemed impertinent—if not downright obnoxious—for a newcomer to write a tour guide to a place she was only beginning to know. But, encouraged by friends and colleagues, I spent a happy year doing just that.

In that time, Montgomery—fictionalized so evocatively by the Fitzgeralds as Tarleton and Jeffersonville in their books—became a home and a treasured subject of study. Despite all the havoc caused by short-sighted developers and interstate highway construction, remnants of Zelda and Scott's city are still here. The result is a guide that I hope connects readers to the town that brought this iconic couple together and, perhaps, gave them their happiest and most nostalgic memories.

Wouldn't you like to smell the pine woods of Alabama again? You were a young lieutenant and I was a fragrant phantom, wasn't I? And it was a radiant night, a night of soft conspiracy and the trees agreed that it was all going to be for the best.

— ZELDA FITZGERALD,
Dear Scott, Dearest Zelda

Tour Routes

ALABAMA RIVER

I-65 TO BIRMINGHAM

13 WATER ST.

MOLTON

TALLAPOOSA

COMMERCE

COOSA

COURT

14

Tour 2: Downtown

MAXWELL BLVD.

CLAY ST.

65

HERRON ST.

I-65 TO MOBILE

MARTHA

BIBB

CATOMA

WILKINSON

MONTGOMERY

12

11

10

COURT

LEE

CHURCH

7

6

CLAYTON

ALAB

SC

MOBILE

Tour 1: Zelda's Neighborhood

5

4

GOLDTHWAITE

CAROLINE

HALCOMBE

SAYRE

MILDRED

2

PLEASANT

1

3

I-85 TO ATLANTA

20 SAYRE

COURT

W JEFF DAVIS

HANN

N
W — E
S

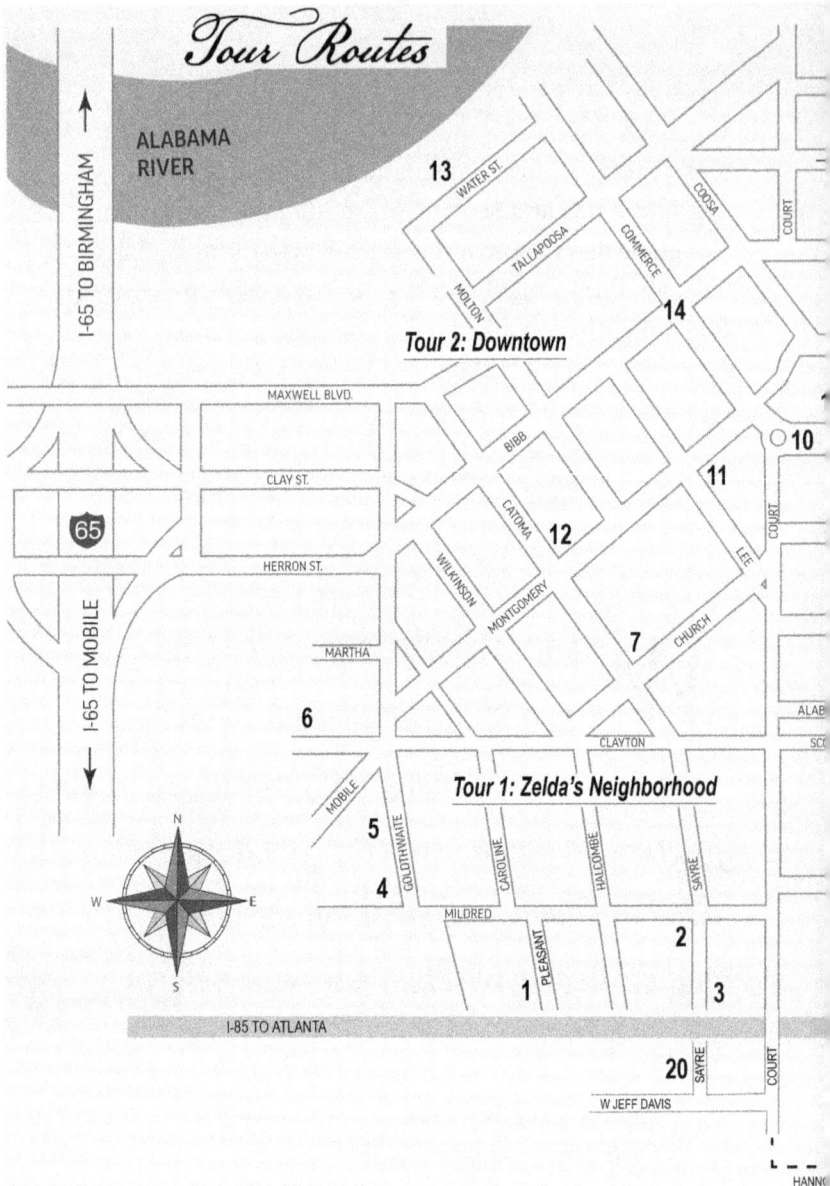

Tour 3: Cloverdale

This portion of the map is not to scale,
and locations 22–26 are further west than
indicated by map position.

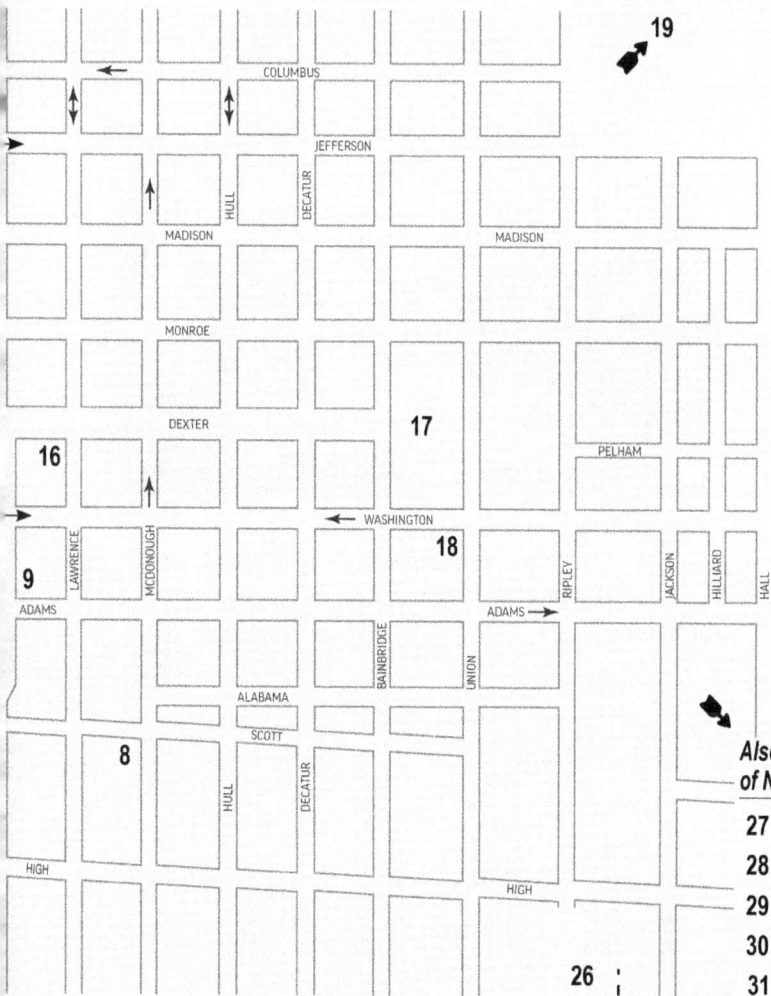

19

COLUMBUS

JEFFERSON

MADISON   MADISON

MONROE

DEXTER   17

16   PELHAM

LAWRENCE   MCDONOUGH   HULL   DECATUR   ← WASHINGTON

9   18

ADAMS   ADAMS →

RIPLEY   JACKSON   HILLIARD   HALL

ALABAMA
SCOTT
8
HULL   DECATUR   BAINBRIDGE   UNION

*Also
of Note*

27

28

HIGH   HIGH   29

30

26   31

I-85 TO ATLANTA

21
JULIA

HULL
FOREST

PINELEAF

25
CARTER HILL

23
22
FELDER

BOULTIER   COLLEGE STREET

24
FAIRVIEW

Motor magazine published this 1920 photo of F. Scott and Zelda Sayre Fitzgerald, about to depart in their "rolling junk"—a 1918 Marmon—on a road trip from Westport, Connecticut, to Montgomery.

*T*he sunlight dripped over the house
  like golden paint over an art jar, and
the freckling shadows here and there only
intensified the rigor of the bath of light.

— F. Scott Fitzgerald, using the Sayre
   home on Pleasant Street in "The Ice Palace"

Tour 1: Zelda's Neighborhood

The Sayres lived in one of Montgomery's oldest residential areas, just a few blocks south of downtown. The neighborhood, known for its Victorian Queen Anne architecture, declined after 1960 but is gradually being redeveloped.

1. Sayre Family Home

500 Block of Pleasant Avenue

Zelda Sayre's childhood home was at 6 Pleasant Avenue (the city has since renumbered the streets). It was built on the remains of the Wilson Plantation which fell into disrepair following the Civil War and Reconstruction. The Sayre home was demolished in the 1970s, despite the efforts of daughter Scottie Fitzgerald Smith to save it. What remains is an enclosed grassy lot and a partial stone staircase visible behind a chain-link fence. F. Scott Fitzgerald was once photographed on these steps.

Happily, next door to the empty lot sits a white frame structure, ca. 1900, that appears to be a replica of the Sayre house. The surviving house features a front porch that suggests where the teenage Zelda would have received her many suitors and entertained her future husband. The Sayre household included Zelda's three sisters, Majorie, Rosalind, and Clothilde, and brother Tony, the parents, and various relatives from both sides of her family. Her father, Anthony, a justice of the Alabama Supreme Court, refused to have a mortgage and so rented his Pleasant

This is not the Sayre home but is next door to where the house stood and is of similar architecture.

Avenue home from descendants of the Wilsons until his death in 1931. Zelda wrote that the house "had an affinity for light." Her front bedroom overlooked a pear orchard that was all that remained of the Wilson Plantation.

> . . . **Go north on Pleasant, turn right on Mildred, then right on Sayre.**

2. Sayre Street School
506 Sayre Street

The corner of Mildred and Sayre streets had long been the site of several nineteenth-century schools including the Chilton College, established in 1866 and named for William Parish Chilton, the cousin of Zelda's mother,

*F*lushed with the heat of palpitant cheeks, the school room swung from the big square windows and anchored itself into a dismal lithograph of the signing of the Declaration of Independence.

— ZELDA FITZGERALD, *Save Me the Waltz*

Minnie Machen Sayre. Chilton College evolved into the Montgomery Female College (from which Minnie Sayre graduated), but as the population grew, it was decided the facility was inadequate. In its place, a "handsome and modern" structure was built by J. W. Worthington in 1891 and named the Sayre Street School. The Victorian Romanesque result certainly filled the bill. It has a pretty multi-colored brick facade with decorative stone bands above the six over six windows. The interior appears to have the original wood floors with east and west halls divided into four classrooms. The school was closed in 1976 and it last served as a florist shop.

Zelda began attending the Sayre Street School in 1906 at the age of six. Her father, Judge Anthony D. Sayre, served on the Montgomery Board of Education and felt his daughter should attend public school (rigidly segregated by race in Alabama until the 1960s). She returned home on her first day to proclaim that she "seem(ed) to know everything" and refused to go back. Zelda's mother acquiesced to her daughter's whim and kept her home for another year.

. . . Travel a half block further south on Sayre Street.

3. Margaret Booth School for Girls
529 Sayre Street

This now privately owned building is an American Foursquare with a center doorway and double porch columns typical to the area's architecture. The hexagonal concrete block sidewalks leading up to it are often seen in the oldest sections of Montgomery. This was Miss Margaret Booth's home when she established the school in 1914. Educated at Mount Holyoke in Massachusetts, Booth returned to Montgomery to serve many years as a teacher and principal in the public school system. She was considered a leading local intellectual and according to her 1953 obituary was "an ardent student of European culture, making annual summer tours of that continent."

The school had a classic liberal arts curriculum including art history, languages, geography, and history. It had an excellent academic reputation and served as a feeder school to many eminent northeastern colleges for women. At one point, Zelda's friend from childhood, the writer Sara Haardt, administered the history department. Sara would later marry the cultural critic and newspaper editor H. L. Mencken. The school closed upon Miss Booth's death.

Zelda was not a student of Miss Booth but many of her friends were. As a youth she occasionally attended the school's plays, ducking out when she grew bored. The Fitzgeralds' daughter, Scottie Fitzgerald Smith, was enrolled in the school from 1931 to 1932 after the family repatriated from Europe and came to Montgomery in part due to Judge Anthony Sayre's declining health. Despite the Booth School's sterling reputation, Scottie wrote in her memoir: ". . . we studied the War Between the States to the exclusion, as I remember, of just about every other period in history . . . it wasn't until I got to school in the North that I found out that we had lost the war and then I had to relearn my history."

. . . Return to Mildred, turn left, and go west for three blocks to Goldthwaite.

4. Winter Place
Northwest corner of Goldthwaite and Mildred streets

This National Register mansion is actually two houses joined together to form a cohesive whole. The North House was built in 1855 by Colonel J. S. Winter and is in the popular Victorian Italianate style designed by architect Samuel Sloan of Philadelphia. It features a tower with a mansard roof, arched doorways and windows, and is connected by a windowed corridor to the Second Empire style South House. The interiors of both wings

Winter Place, ca. 1900.

have sweepingly high ceilings with massive wooden doors and tall pier mirrors.

In Scott and Zelda's lifetimes, Winter Place was owned by the Thorington family. It has often been suggested that this is where Zelda met Lieutenant Fitzgerald at an afternoon tea although it is more likely that the meeting was at the Montgomery Country Club on Carter Hill Road. Zelda was a good friend of owner Bessie Thorington and in March 1943, she visited the home and met Thorington's nephew, Winter Thorington, a boarding school friend of the author Gore Vidal. According to Winter, "there was a bit of electricity in Zelda that I enjoyed being around. She was very worldly and I thought quite intelligent. She had a magnetic personality."

Winter Place declined after World War II into

Bohemian squalor and was chopped up into many apartments, where lived a revolving cast of young law clerks, newspaper reporters, and civil rights workers. Wild parties held in the complex are legendary. After many years of neglect, Winter Place was being renovated and as of 2021 the south wing was already occupied by the current owner. This magnificent structure hints at the past grandeur of the neighborhood that is now being revitalized.

> . . . **Continue north on Goldthwaite Street for a long half-block.**

*T*he Ford . . . rattled down Valley Avenue into Jefferson Street where the dust road became a pavement; along opiate Millicent Place, where there were half a dozen prosperous, substantial mansions.

— F. Scott Fitzgerald, using Winter Place
in "The Ice Palace"

5. Church of the Holy Comforter

(Today, The Sanctuary at the Jubilee Center) 432 Goldthwaite Street

The Sayre family worshipped at this former Episcopal church, consecrated in June 1887. Zelda's mother, Minnie Machen Sayre, sang in the choir and Zelda was baptized here in 1910. In the 1940s, she attended Sunday services and was often seen exiting the church carrying her bible. The church is an example of rustic Carpenter Gothic architecture and retains its original heart-pine exterior with pointed arches and board and batten siding. Much of the interior was removed in 1959 to the congregation's new church building on Woodley Road. The arched stained glass windows were replaced by clear panes. A photo of the original sanctuary hangs inside near the front door.

The Church of the Holy Comforter, as it would have looked during Zelda's time.

The building was converted into a playhouse and for many years served as the home of the Montgomery Little Theatre. That group disbanded after the Alabama Shakespeare Festival opened in the 1980s, and today the structure is operated by a nonprofit organization as The Sanctuary—a venue for musical and theatrical events.

> **. . . Continue on Goldthwaite to Clayton Street. Turn left for three-quarters of a block.**

6. Scottie Smith property
440 Clayton Street

In 1973, the Fitzgeralds' only child, Scottie Fitzgerald Smith, relocated to Montgomery from Washington, D.C., so she could take care of Zelda's older sister, Rosalind Sayre Smith, who then lived on South Perry Street. Scottie purchased and lived in a house on Gilmer Avenue in the Garden District until her death in 1986. A journalist and political activist, she was also committed to preserving her mother's old neighborhood. To that end, when Cottage Hill redevelopment began in the 1970s, she pitched in and bought a handsome house at 440 Clay Street so it could be saved and renovated. The house has tall columns supporting a flat roof that overhangs banistered double front porches that span the width of both stories.

> **. . . Return east on Clayton Street for three blocks then turn left on Holcombe Street to Catoma Street.**

7. Catoma Street Church of Christ/Zelda's roller-skating routes

100 Catoma Street

The well-preserved Catoma Church of Christ was completed in 1862 as Temple Beth-Or, for the congregation Kahl Montgomery, which outgrew the structure by 1902. Young Zelda would have roller skated by here and also down other nearby streets. The slopes were a test of courage for children, and Zelda was expert at navigating them. She once saved a younger friend from serious injury by overtaking her as she careened towards the uneven cobblestones at the foot of the former synagogue. Another skating route for early twentieth-century children was over the rolling hills of South/North Perry Street. Zelda often latched onto drays or carts for the return journey, another tribute to her daredevil spirit.

> . . . Go south on Catoma for one block to Clayton, then turn left and go east for four blocks (Clayton becomes Scott when it crosses Court) to one-way McDonough (you can't turn right).

This is April again. Roller skates rain slowly down the street.

— F. SCOTT FITZGERALD, *The Note-Books*

Early postcard view of where Zelda went to high school and became a belle.

8. Sidney Lanier High School

(Today, Baldwin Arts and Academics Magnet School) 410 S. Mc-Donough Street

Named for the popular Southern poet who lived in Montgomery from 1865 to 1867 and designed by renowned architect Frank Lockwood, this Gothic Revival building opened its doors in 1910. Today, its interior remains mostly intact with an auditorium, original hardwood floors, ornamental iron staircases, and massive brick fireplaces featuring classical bas-relief moldings and terra cotta insets. The former gymnasium is now a dance studio dedicated to Zelda Fitzgerald.

Zelda attended the school from 1914 until her graduation in May 1918. Here she first established herself as one of Montgomery's premiere belles. She was voted the prettiest and most attractive girl in her class and her mouth was chosen for the composite picture of the ideal Senior girl. On March 22, 1918, she appeared in the auditorium as "War" in a patriotic pageant that was so successful it played again a few weeks later. Unfortunately, at that performance, Zelda forgot her lines. After an awkward pause she announced to the bemused audience that she "had been permanently interrupted." She left the stage to laughter and applause. At graduation, she flouted the five-dollar limit on dresses and arrived wearing a chiffon dress with a sweeping, wide-brimmed hat. For that infraction, she sat in the audience instead of onstage with her classmates. Biographer Nancy Milford reported that Zelda's friend Irby Jones swore "that she was laughing at them all."

In 1929, a grander and larger Sidney Lanier High School opened in the Garden District on South Court Street and its original building became the Baldwin junior high school. In the 1980s, Baldwin became a successful magnet middle school for young artists and scholars in the Montgomery County public school system.

> **. . . Return west on Scott for two blocks then turn right onto one-way Perry Street.**

9. Carnegie Library

(Now a county office) 131 South Perry Street

This is a fine example of the three thousand free public libraries spread throughout the United States in the late nineteenth and early twentieth centuries by steel magnate

Library of Congress photo of the Carnegie Library, ca. 1906.

and philanthropist Andrew Carnegie. Designed in the grandiose Beaux-Arts style, the Montgomery edifice boasts monumental granite columns, Palladian-style windows, and balustraded balconies. Its interior features ornamental iron stair handrails, marble columns, and large, airy rooms. The library was designed by the New York City architectural firm of York and Sawyer and built by Laurie and Cook Construction Company. Today, it is home to the city's Property Appraisal Office.

In 1902, the Montgomery Library Association, spearheaded by the Reverend Edgar Gardner Murphy of St. John's Episcopal Church, raised funds to purchase land for the proposed library at South Perry and Adams streets. Murphy was a strong supporter of textile workers, an advocate for child labor laws, a committed activist for African American enfranchisement, and a believer in universal education. With the latter in mind, he approached Carnegie, who committed to donating $50,000 if Montgomery would provide $5,000 in matching funds. The agreement was met, the library was completed, and it opened in 1904.

As a child, Zelda was a voracious reader (she claimed to have read all "the rough passages" of Boccaccio's *Decameron*). She visited the library and checked out books on subjects she loved, including historical fiction and biographies of Civil War officers. It is likely that in 1931, Scott, a doting father, would have introduced his ten-year-old daughter, Scottie, to the library; she said her father enjoyed sharing his favorite books with her, including *Ivanhoe* and *Great Expectations*.

Later in her life, Zelda became friends with head research librarian Juliette Hampton Morgan and her mother, Lila Bess Morgan. Zelda visited them at their home, bringing gifts of flowers and fruit from her own garden. (Juliette would be remembered as a vocal white supporter of the 1955–56 bus boycott—paying a huge price when she was shunned by her friends and community and driven from her job. She committed suicide in 1957, leaving a note that "I can't go on." The present main city library at Lawrence and High streets was eventually named in her honor.)

In nonchalant tones we explained . . . that we were touring to Alabama. "My golly!" exclaimed one of the onlookers in an awed voice, "That's way down in Virginia, isn't it?"

— F. SCOTT FITZGERALD,
  "The Cruise of the Rolling Junk"

*M*ontgomery is as green and fragrant and as ingratiating as it was so many years ago.

— ZELDA FITZGERALD,
Dear Scott, Dearest Zelda

Tour 2: Downtown

The political and cultural center of Montgomery, the state capital of Alabama

10. Dexter Avenue/Court Square Fountain

Court Square is located at the western end of the wide, sweeping avenue that leads to the Capitol. Originally named Market Street, the name was changed in 1884 to honor Andrew Dexter, the founder of the early nineteenth-century settlement of New Philadelphia that merged on December 13, 1819, with another village, Alabama Town, to become the town of Montgomery (named for a different general than the county's namesake).

At the center of Court Square is a majestic 1885 cast-iron fountain, which stands over an old artesian well. The sculpture was cast by J. L. Mott Ironworks of New York, then overhauled in 1984 by Robinson Iron of Alexander City, Alabama. At its apex stands the mythical Hebe, cupbearer to the Greek gods and the goddess of eternal youth. She is attended by children, servants bearing hand towels, and preening cranes rather than the traditional eagles. As a child, Zelda was known to play at the fountain.

It was on Dexter that as a popular teenager, seated in the rumble seat of a jalopy while wearing her famous flesh-colored Annette Kellerman bathing suit, she greeted a group of male admirers by jumping up, stretching her arms wide, and exclaiming "All my jellies!" (slang for the local swains). Despite long-standing local lore, there is no evidence that Zelda ever jumped into or swam in the fountain.

Shortly after the Fitzgeralds married and Scott had produced the best-selling novel *This Side of Paradise,* the couple returned to Montgomery from their home in Connecticut. Zelda was hungry for the peaches and biscuits served in Southern kitchens. According to Fitzgerald, as soon as they drove towards the entrance to the city "we were in Montgomery—it was breathless, unbelievable. . . why Montgomery was on another plane and we were actually rolling into it, right down Dexter Avenue as though it had been a street in Westport!" They had made the five-day trip in their rolling junk (a 1918 Marmon automobile) only to find that Zelda's parents had taken the train north to Connecticut to surprise them.

. . . From the fountain, turn west onto Montgomery Street and go to the end of the first block.

11. Elite Cafe
121 Montgomery Street

An institution in Montgomery and Alabama from 1911 until it closed in 1990, its unchanged 1960s exterior can still be observed. The restaurant was popular with both the Sayre and Fitzgerald family.

The Elite was owned by a Greek immigrant family, the Xides, and featured some mid-twentieth-century dishes such as Oysters Rockefeller and Trout Amandine. The

A picture postcard composite of interior and exterior views of what was once one of Alabama's most famous restaurants.

1931 menu that would have been served to the Fitzgeralds included dishes such as Au Gratin Macaroni, Broiled Spanish Mackerel, and Swedish Salad—the latter a dish that might feature cold seafood and vegetables. Along with its delicious food and attractive Art Deco interior, its distinguishing feature may have been the local pronunciation of its name—*Ee-lite* rather than *Ee-leet*. According to Sara Mayfield, a Montgomery friend of the Fitzgeralds and their biographer, the mispronunciation was due to it being of Greek origin (meaning joy) rather than the more familiar French derivation. A longtime resident of Montgomery says that Zelda herself came up with this unique explanation because she was tired of Scott's complaints about how locals pronounced the word.

. . . Continue two blocks west on Montgomery Street.

12. Jefferson Davis Hotel

(Today, King-Williams Apartments) 344 Montgomery Street

This splendid building was erected in 1929 by Alabama's Hugger Brothers Construction Company and was part of a Southern hotel chain created by Carling L. Dinkler. Noted local architect Frederick Ausfeld gave the hotel a neoclassical style. Ausfeld, of German origin, designed many significant buildings in Montgomery, including the grand 1929 Sidney Lanier High School.

The Jefferson Davis Hotel had 250 rooms and baths with "circulating ice water," radios in every room, and a coffee shop. When the Fitzgeralds returned to Montgomery in 1931 they chose to stay here before moving to their Old Cloverdale rental home. According to their essay "Show Mr. and Mrs. F. to Number—," they paid nine dollars for three rooms and four baths "so the bellboys would have some place to sleep when we rang for them."

The hotel was also a stone's throw from their favorite

Nothing had happened since the Civil War. Everybody had forgotten why the hotel had been erected . . .

— F. Scott and Zelda Fitzgerald,
"Show Mr. and Mrs. F. to Number—"

JEFFERSON DAVIS HOTEL, MONTGOMERY, ALA.—41

Picture postcard from the 1920s.

Montgomery restaurant, the Elite Cafe, and an easy stroll from Union Station and the downtown stores and movie theaters.

From the outside, the hotel appears unchanged. Inside, it has been converted to subsidized apartment units and has been renamed the King-Williams Apartments (country music legend Hank Williams reportedly performed live in the hotel, and the Reverend Martin Luther King Jr. preached sermons over WSFA radio, which once had a broadcast studio in the building).

> **. . . Turn right onto Catoma Street, go north one block to Bibb. Turn right on Bibb and go one block, then turn left on Molton. Go north two blocks, then turn right onto Water Street.**

. . . and on to the downtown section. Driving was perilous here, for it was shopping time.

— F. Scott Fitzgerald, using
Montgomery memories in "The Ice Palace"

Picture postcard from the early 1900s. One of the famed "Lightning Route" electric streetcars sits in the foreground.

13. Union Station

300 Water Street

One of Montgomery's most distinguished buildings, with its accompanying six-hundred-foot-long train shed, sits on the Alabama River next to busy Commerce Street. The station was built by the Louisville & Nashville Railroad engineering department in 1898 and was served by six railroad lines. The station and the shed, the latter with an architecturally significant type of metal roof truss, combine Chateauesque and Romanesque architectural styles.

In a March 1919 letter to Scott, Zelda, who enjoyed pranks, wrote: "Yesterday, when the University boys took their belated departure, John Sellers wheeled me thru a vast throng of people at the station, crying intermittently 'the lady hasn't walked in five years.' We had collected fo'

*T*he David Knights stepped out of the old brick station. The Southern town slept soundless on the wide palette of the cotton fields.

— Zelda Fitzgerald,
  using Union Station in *Save Me the Waltz*

bits when our innocent past-time was rudely interrupted by a somewhat brawny arm-of-the-law being thrust between me and the rolling chair . . ." She was escorted out of the station.

In March 1920 Zelda Sayre, accompanied by her older sister Marjorie, departed to marry F. Scott Fitzgerald in New York City. Zelda wore a gray traveling suit, and biographer Kendall Taylor records the words of sister Rosalind Sayre Smith: "Zelda's friends, carrying bouquets for her, went to the station to see her off . . . Several years ago I was introduced to a Montgomery woman and mentioned as Zelda's sister. 'I did not know Zelda personally,' she said, 'but I happened to see her in the station the morning she was leaving for her marriage, and I've never forgotten how beautiful she was.'"

Before the marriage, Scott worked at an unsatisfactory advertising job in New York City while conducting a long-distance romance with Zelda. To reassure himself of her love and fidelity, he would occasionally take the train from New York's Pennsylvania Station to Montgomery's Union Station and then a taxi to her home on Pleasant Avenue. Reunited, they would sit before the fireplace while Judge Sayre kept a wary eye on them.

Union Station ended rail passenger service in 1979. Today the structure hosts restaurants, private businesses, and one unique workshop-residence of a luthier.

> **. . . Continue east until Water dead-ends into Commerce. The pedestrian tunnel beneath the adjacent railroad tracks leads to the riverfront.**

I love you with all my heart because you are my own girl and that is all I know.

— F. Scott Fitzgerald, undated letter

14. Commerce Street

Once a thriving business and commercial artery to the Alabama River, the wide, median-divided Commerce Street stretches only three blocks to Hebe's Fountain at Court Square. Prior to the Civil War, cotton and slaves were warehoused along the street awaiting auction; today the street is mostly trafficked by tourists and local profes-sionals occupying the repurposed commercial structures.

The east side of Commerce retains its nineteenth- and early twentieth-century cast-iron building fronts with their spectacularly arched entryways and windows. Dates and names are delightfully inscribed across the pink, tan, and red brick facades. The 1891 Steiner Lobman Building, in particular, interests with its statue of Athena perched on the roof. She stands before an ornate Victorian casket that once hid a water tower. The stately 1906 Hobbie Building, originally the home of the Hobbie Grocery Company, stands by the riverfront. The prominent Hobbies were involved in numerous local businesses. One wonders if Fitzgerald, in his many train arrivals at the adjacent Union

Looking south on Commerce Street in 1919. Zelda was among the women in the foreground welcoming returning veterans.

A nd now the young men began drifting back from the ends of the earth—some with Canadian uniforms, some with crutches or empty sleeves. A returned battalion of the National Guard paraded through the street with open ranks for their dead…

— F. SCOTT FITZGERALD,
"The Last of the Belles"

Station, was inspired, despite the difference in spelling, to give that surname to his jaded Hollywood anti-hero in *The Pat Hobby Stories*.

On May 12, 1919, Zelda was one of the rainbow-gowned girls lining Commerce to greet the returning World War I veterans of the Rainbow Division of the 167th Infantry. She also served candy, cake, and cigarettes to the men. Her photo was on the front page of the *Montgomery Advertiser* the next day.

> **… Proceed to the south end of Commerce at Court Square and turn left onto Dexter Avenue.**

15. Montgomery Fair

(Today, Rosa Parks pocket park) 39 Dexter Avenue

Montgomery Fair was a four-floor department store founded in 1908. It had entrances on Dexter Avenue and Court and Monroe streets. Over the years, it went through several architectural and structural changes and all that remains is the upper façade of the 1940 renovation featuring an art deco panel of glass blocks. The Fair closed in the 1960s after shopping malls had opened in the suburbs to the south and east. Today, its location features an enclosed public pocket park where tourists and residents sit and chat while sipping caffé lattes and chai teas served up at the adjoining Prevail Union coffee shop.

In early December 1931, Zelda went Christmas shopping at Montgomery Fair with her young daughter, Scottie. There, she experienced a typical event in the life of a mother: she lost Scottie in the milling crowd. That morning, Zelda had given her daughter permission to shop on her own with specific instructions to meet again at a certain place within the store. Instead, Scottie returned to their car while the panicked Zelda searched for her. She wrote to Scott in California: ". . . it was ghastly like being whirled through endless rotating hypotheses of life and being in some chaotic functioning of the consciousness without the mind." One can only imagine the eventual reunion in the car!

Of course, Montgomery Fair is most famous for one of its employees, the seamstress Rosa Parks. At 6 p.m.

on December 1, 1955, she left her work in the Fair's alterations department headed outside to Court Square, where she boarded the Cleveland Avenue bus for the two-mile ride to her apartment. City bus seating was then segregated, and two blocks along the bus route Parks was arrested for violating Montgomery's segregation ordinance after she refused to surrender her seat and move to the back of the bus. Thus she entered the history books as an American heroine. Parks worked at Montgomery Fair for only two years in the 1950s so she would never have sewn garments for the Sayres or Fitzgeralds. But Zelda Fitzgerald and Rosa Parks were only a decade apart in age, and Montgomery was then a small place; they could have unknowingly passed each

The Fair, as Zelda would have known it, on Dexter Avenue.

other on the streets of downtown, one a future civil rights icon, the other a future cultural icon.

. . . Continue east on Dexter for another block.

16. Chris' Hot Dogs

138 Dexter Avenue

Chris' Hot Dogs is a beloved mainstay in Montgomery and its oldest continuously operating restaurant. Opened in 1917 by the Greek immigrant Christopher Anastastios Katechis, the narrow establishment has been serving hamburgers and hot dogs with the special chili sauce for more than a century. Now owned by father and son Theo and Gus Katechis, the restaurant has fed everyone from Hank Williams to Elvis Presley to Presidents Franklin Roosevelt and George H. W. Bush. According to the Katechises, Martin Luther King Jr. often stopped by in the early hours to purchase a morning newspaper. Earlier, Scott, Zelda, and Scottie were regular customers, lining up for a hot dog and Coke whenever they were in town.

When Zelda returned to Montgomery in the 1930s and 1940s, she resumed dance lessons at local studios, including one directly above Chris' owned by William F. Pinkston, known to his friends as Billy. After class, Zelda and other dancers would repair to Chris' Hot Dogs for a late-night snack.

. . . Continue east to the end of Dexter at what is known locally as Goat Hill.

Ca. 1940s postcard of the Alabama Capitol.

17. Alabama State Capitol

600 Dexter Avenue

This impressive building was erected in 1850–51 on the foundations of the 1847 capitol that was burned by a suspected arsonist in 1849. In 1861 the Confederate States of America was created by delegates meeting in the chamber of the state house of representatives. The building also housed the Alabama Supreme Court until the mid-twentieth century.

According to the Fitzgeralds' friend and biographer, Sara Mayfield, Zelda, along with her friend, Tallulah "Dutch" Bankhead, held court as children on the portico and stairs and the steep incline of Goat Hill. They turned cartwheels and performed backflips and raced about on roller skates. The Capitol was one of the first tourist sites that Zelda showed Scott Fitzgerald when they were courting—taking him to the gold star embedded in the Dexter-facing west portico's marble floor marking where Jefferson Davis stood while being inaugurated as president of the Confederacy.

Zelda's father, Judge Anthony Sayre, had his office on the second floor in the East Wing of the Capitol. He served as a justice of the Alabama Supreme Court for twenty-five years and was considered a brilliant jurist. He nevertheless was the author of the 1892–93 Sayre Election Law that disenfranchised illiterate poor whites

- -

She was slender and athletic, without underdevelopment, and it was a delight to watch her move about a room, walk along a street, swing a golf club, or turn a "cartwheel."

— F. Scott Fitzgerald, channeling Zelda's childhood in *This Side of Paradise*

From his grave the dome of the Capitol blotted out the setting sun.

— Zelda Fitzgerald, *Save Me the Waltz*

- -

and African Americans by having the state rather than political parties distribute ballots and listing candidates by alphabetical order rather than by symbols and colors. In her autobiographic novel *Save Me the Waltz*, Zelda poignantly recounts clearing out the judge's office after his death in 1931. She found no clue to her austere father's inner life from his personal effects. She wrote, "He must have forgot to leave the message."

> **. . . Turn right on Bainbridge Street and go one block to the southwest corner of Union and Washington streets.**

18. Sayre House

(Today, White House of the Confederacy Museum) 644 Washington Avenue

Local merchant William Sayre, the great-uncle of Zelda Fitzgerald, built this house between 1832 and 1835. Originally in the federal style, a new owner, Colonel Joseph Winter, converted it to the popular Italianate design in 1855. The house once stood at the corner of Bibb and Lee streets but was moved by the First White House Association to its present location in 1921.

The Jefferson Davis family occupied the house for a few months in the spring of 1861 before the CSA government relocated to Richmond, Virginia. Most of the decorative items on display in the "First White House" belonged to the Davis family. Several exceptions were donated by Scottie Fitzgerald Smith who inherited them

The former Sayre family home later occupied by Jefferson Davis.

from her grandmother, Minnie Machen Sayre. They include two handsome red velvet "lady and gentleman" chairs and a tall, ornate secretary that was damaged during the Civil War when a Union gunboat shelled Mineral Mount, the Kentucky plantation home of the Machen family. The secretary is mentioned in *Save Me the Waltz* as a talisman of rebellion. These items are located in the rear hallway near the gift shop. A small card table that belonged to William Sayre can be seen in the second-floor hallway across from the nursery.

> . . . Turn left on Union and go north for three blocks, turn right onto Jefferson, go east for a quarter mile, then turn left behind the police station onto North Jackson for one block to Columbus. (Slightly off the route map on page 11.)

19. Oakwood Cemetery

829 Columbus Street

In the early nineteenth century, this large, evocative cemetery was built in what was then the northeast fringes of Montgomery. The cemetery's original designation as a free burying ground helps explain its "irregularity of lot shapes and sizes and the haphazard arrangement of graves." Nevertheless, it is beautifully situated on hilly terrain overlooking downtown. Oakwood includes Catholic (St. Margaret's), Jewish, and African American sections, a potter's field, and Confederate and Union cemeteries as well as a section for French and British airmen who died during pilot training at Maxwell Field during World War II. Oakwood is the final resting place of many prominent Montgomerians including early resident William Sayre, Zelda's great-uncle, former governor William Oates ("he gave his right arm for the cause"), and singer Hank Williams and his first wife, Audrey.

Sayre Plot, Lot 7, Square 51, Survey 3, entrance of St. Mary's

This is the final resting place of Judge Anthony D. Sayre Sr., his wife, Minnie, and sons Daniel and Anthony D. Sayre Jr. Also included in the enclosed plot are Zelda's grandparents Daniel Sayre and Musidora Morgan Sayre. A newly installed plaque is in memoriam to F. Scott and Zelda Fitzgerald and daughter Scottie Fitzgerald Smith and acknowledges that the three are buried in St. Mary's Churchyard, Rockville, Maryland.

Wreford Mausoleum, Lot 3, Square 33, Survey 2, main entrance

William Wreford, a Confederate soldier who died in 1864, is entombed in a brick mausoleum built into a steep, grassy incline. Today, it is simply marked with the words "Wreford 1866."

The grave has significance in the life of both Fitzgeralds. In the spring of 1919, Zelda and a group of friends descended upon Oakwood Cemetery and found this old vault. Engulfed in pathos at the death of this young soldier, she wrote a passionate letter to Fitzgerald that reads in

The William Wreford tomb (photo by Alaina Doten).

Occasionally they saw a kneeling figure with tributary flowers, but over most of the graves lay silence and withered leaves with only the fragrance that their own shadowy memories could waken in living minds.

— F. Scott Fitzgerald, "The Ice Palace"

part: "I've spent today in the graveyard—it really isn't a cemetery, you know, trying to unlock a rusty iron vault . . . It's all washed and covered with weepy, watery blue flowers that might have grown from dead eyes—sticky to touch with a sickening odor—the boys wanted to test my nerve tonight—I wanted to *feel* William Wreford, 1864." The letter goes on to speculate about her own future grave and how people might ponder the color of her eyes. She concludes "old death is so beautiful—so very beautiful— We will die together—I know." Fitzgerald was so struck by the imagery and beauty of her language he sent her a large, feathered fan as a gift. He then incorporated her letter (calling the soldier William Dayfield) into the final pages of his first novel, *This Side of Paradise.*

Mama's little house is so sunshine-y and so full of grace; the moated mornings remind me of twenty-five years ago when life was as full of promise as it now is of memory . . . Mama is the best and most gracious of company. We linger over things: peaches and figs and the poignant fragrances of a summer already on the wane . . .

— ZELDA FITZGERALD,
  Dear Scott, Dearest Zelda

Tour 3: Old Cloverdale / Hazel Hedge / Oak Park

*Old Cloverdale is a landscaped midtown neigh-
borhood that was once a separate incorporated
town before its merger with the City of Montgomery in 1927. It has been suggested that Old
Cloverdale was designed by Frederick Law Olmsted, landscape architect of Central Park in New
York City. Olmsted was in Montgomery during
the late nineteenth century (working on the State
Capitol grounds) but no documentation proves
that he was involved in the suburb's development.
Cloverdale was originally called Graham's Woods
or The Pines because of its thicket of virgin pine
interspersed with meadows of clover.*

20. Rabbit Run

Sayre Street, between West Jeff Davis Avenue and the south side
of Interstate 85

After the death of Judge Anthony Sayre in 1931,
Zelda's mother, Minnie Machen Sayre, gave up the rental
home on Pleasant and moved to Sayre Street next door
to her daughter, Marjorie Sayre Brinson. Mrs. Sayre's
small bungalow was nicknamed Rabbit Run. In 1940,
Zelda returned to live with her mother. While spending
a good deal of her time gardening and painting on the

Minnie Machen Sayre in the Rabbit Run parlor, right, and on its front porch, facing page. Both photos are courtesy of the F. Scott and Zelda Fitzgerald Museum.

patio, she also lectured (perhaps on ballet) at Huntingdon College, reviewed books for Armed Forces Radio, and was an active member of Pen Women.

Sayre Street was split north and south during the construction of Interstate Highway 85, and Rabbit Run was razed. All that remains of Zelda's last home is a fenced yard overlooking the interstate. According to former journalist May Lamar, writing in the *Montgomery Advertiser* in 1984, beyond the fence one could see mimosa trees, honeysuckle, and kiss-me-at-the-gate. Today the yard is a shaded jungle of vegetation and unpruned trees.

Attractive intact bungalows from Zelda's time can be seen on Sayre Street.

> Return to West Jeff Davis Street, go left for a half
> block to Court Street, then go right on Court for three
> blocks, turn left on East Hannon for one block, then
> left on Perry for one block, then right onto Julia Street
> to the middle of the first block.

21. Montgomery Little Theatre

130 Julia Street, between Lawrence and Perry streets

This Tudor Revival house with mullion windows and end gables was once the home of Montgomery's community theater. Jean Read, of Hazel Hedge, was a founding member of the troupe. Its theatrical seasons featured sophisticated fare. The company staged Noel Coward's *Hay Fever*, *Arms and the Man* by George Bernard Shaw, *The Circle* by Somerset Maugham, and, incredibly, *Lysistrata* by Aristophanes.

When the Fitzgeralds were living in town in 1931, Zelda was approached by one of the directors of the theater to star as Amanda in Noel Coward's *Private Lives*. Unfortunately, after mulling it over, she declined the request. Later that year, she rented the building for a children's Christmas show with a plan to serve eggnog and cake to twenty of Scottie's friends. She was approached

*T*he real plot of all Little Theatre plays…is how the young gosling actor of fourteen ever managed to be in love with the leading woman of forty . . .

— F. Scott Fitzgerald, *The Note-Books*

again in 1940 to stage her "farce-fantasy" play *Scandal-abra*. It had been produced in 1933 in Baltimore, where it ran for more than five hours before Scott stepped in to cut it down to a reasonable theatrical length. Sadly, it appears that after the initial interest in Zelda's play, the Montgomery Little Theatre did not produce it. In the 1950s, the company moved to Goldthwaite Street [see location #5 on Tour 1].

> . . . Go east on Julia to Hull, then right for a half mile to Felder, then left for a half mile to Dunbar Street/ Park Avenue. On the right will be Fitzgerald Park and on the left the Fitzgerald Museum.

22. Fitzgerald Park
Felder Avenue and Dunbar Street

This sun-dappled park was dedicated by the Old Cloverdale Association to the memory of the couple on July 14, 1971. Scottie Fitzgerald Smith was present and remarked, "You can't imagine how much it means to me to be here and to have you do this lovely thing for Mama and Daddy." The park features a small fountain, a plaque honoring the couple, a sundial donated by Scottie and paving stones engraved with Zelda's witty and nostalgic quotes. A bench is provided for contemplative sitting.

> . . . Go diagonally across Felder from the park.

*W*e are going to Alabama for the winter and I hope to God I'll finish my novel.

— F. Scott Fitzgerald, correspondence

23. F. Scott and Zelda Fitzgerald Museum
919 Felder Avenue

In the winter of 1931, the Fitzgeralds, in the aftermath of the financial crash that precipitated the Great Depression and ended the Jazz Age, returned to Montgomery from Europe. They took a six-month rental lease in November on this large, cedar-shingled house on Felder Avenue, one of the main arteries of Old Cloverdale. Originally numbered 819, it was built in 1909 (probably designed by architect Frank Lockwood) and featured wide lawns and gardens that produced, in Zelda's words, "little yellow flowers like coins dropped from a worn old purse." The yard is still wide and leafy, with a magnolia and pecan tree dominating the front lawn.

When Fitzgerald was offered an eight-week assignment working on a Jean Harlow movie, he left Alabama for Hollywood. In the interim, Zelda wrote stories, arranged parties and plays for daughter Scottie, and gave her riding and acrobatic lessons. For a short while, Zelda resumed ballet lessons at her friend Amalia Rosenberg's dance studio in downtown. She also looked forward to a Christmas reunion with her family and used the time to create a spectacular holiday display on their sun porch. According to Scottie, the display "opened on Christmas Eve to reveal the history of mankind. The tree stood in the center of the room and around it circled a train, which began in Egypt and stopped at Greece, Rome, the Crusades, the War of the Roses, and so forth. My mother had made tunnels through the Alps out of papier-mâché and a desert with real little palm trees . . ." The author photo of Zelda that was used on the dust jacket of *Save Me the Waltz* was taken in the sun room.

Today, 919 Felder Avenue is an important literary museum due to the efforts of neighbors Julian and Leslie McPhillips, who purchased the house and donated it as a museum to a foundation they created and have guided for many years. The museum houses eleven paintings and pencil drawings by Zelda as well as unpublished family photographs, letters, first editions of the couple's novels, Princeton Triangle Club programs, Minnie Machen Sayre's baby grand piano, and other important artifacts. The most recent acquisition is a facsimile of a brilliant red dress Zelda ordered from a 1949 *Vogue* pattern catalogue.

Other museum activities include literary contests, daily tours, an occasional Charleston dance lesson, and an annual gala. As of this writing, the museum hosts a Great Gatsby exhibit that includes Gatsby's pink suit and

*T*he good things and the first years together, and the good months that we had two years ago in Montgomery will stay with me forever.

— F. Scott Fitzgerald,
Dear Scott, Dearest Zelda

items from the four films made from the novel including the 1974 script by Francis Ford Coppola.

Behind the house is a small garden with a plaque containing a quote from Zelda: "I begin my fall incantation over the seeds and bone meal. There is a starkly epic poetry in even the meagerest of gardening, and I love savoring the fall smoke from burning rubbish and heaping the leaves for earth mold. Though I often wish that it was time to leave for the opera, I am content."

In addition, the museum offers two Airbnbs—the Zelda Suite and the Scott Suite. For rental information, see www.thefitzgeraldmuseum.org.

> **. . . Go east on Felder for one block, then turn right on Boultier and go south until it dead-ends into Fairview. Turn left and go east until Fairview dead-ends.**

24. Montgomery Country Club

Present location is Fairview Avenue at Narrow Lane Road

The Country Club of Montgomery was founded in 1903–04 and has had several locations. One was in a pine grove on Carter Hill Road between Mulberry and West streets. The club's rustic building had elements of the Arts and Crafts movement that is still an architectural feature in the Cloverdale neighborhood. Today, a Sonic Drive-In is in its place. F. Scott Fitzgerald met Zelda Sayre at this location in July 1918. According to Sara Mayfield, he carved their names on the doorpost of the club. Zelda relates in *Save Me the Waltz* that the club burned to the ground shortly after World War I when a stash of corn liquor exploded in the locker room. It actually burned in 1925. The only clue to where it once stood is a side street appropriately named Clubview Road (formerly Seventh Street) which still has homes dating from the era.

Postcard of the original country club, where Scott and Zelda met.

*W*e drank corn on the wings of an
aeroplane in the moon-light and
danced at the country-club.

— Zelda Fitzgerald, *Dear Scott, Dearest Zelda*

The second country club, used by both Scott and Zelda for tennis and golf whenever they were in town during the 1930s, was located where the current club is now, at Narrow Lane Road and Fairview Avenue.

> . . . **Return west on Fairview for two blocks, then turn right on College Street and go north until College crosses Carter Hill Road into Hazel Hedge.**

*T*here was an orchestra—Bingo-Bango
Playing for us to dance the tango
And the people all clapped as we arose
For her sweet face and my new clothes—

— F. Scott Fitzgerald, "Sleeping and Walking," in *Esquire*

25. Hazel Hedge

At Carter Hill and College streets

Today Hazel Hedge is a pretty, wisteria-draped group of privately owned townhouses. Originally the site was the compound and home of prominent Montgomerians Will and Jennie Craik. In 1898, they moved from downtown to what was then a rural outpost. They built a small house and added an orchard, a vegetable garden, chickens and cows, as well as a border of hazelnut trees. When their daughter, Jean, married Nash Read, they extended the house and created a spectacular flower garden.

For decades, the Read house was a gathering place for Montgomery society and its gardens were extolled by interior designers. When the Depression hit, Mrs. Read transformed buildings on the property into rental cottages with fanciful names such as Blandings Castle, Daffodil Cottage, and Casa Baca.

According to her son Nick, when the Fitzgeralds returned to Montgomery in the 1930s, Mrs. Read entertained them with a martini picnic. Interviewed by biographer Nancy Milford in 1965, she reminisced about Zelda's visits during the 1940s. Zelda would bring easel and paints and settle down in the expansive garden for a long afternoon of painting. Zelda favored the more exotic flowers in bloom and would often talk to Mrs. Read about the derivation of plant names. The complex was demolished in the 1970s and the present private homes were built. Today, there is a plaque dedicated to the Craik-Read family.

. . . Exit back to Carter Hill Road, turn right and go west for two blocks to Pineleaf Street, turn right and go north for one block to West Fifth Street. Turn right for one block in front of the school, then left onto Forest Avenue. Go north for a half-mile, crossing over I-85, then watch for the entrance to Oak Park ahead about an eighth of a mile on the left.

26. Oak Park

1010 Forest Avenue

Oak Park today is located on forty acres that were established in the late nineteenth century. It is the oldest park in Montgomery and includes the W. A. Gayle Planetarium, picnic shelters, a playground, and walking trails. Early in the twentieth century, there was a pavilion with a worn dance floor on which "script dances" were held. The names of the prettiest girls were posted at Harry's, a downtown ice cream and soda shop, and boys would sign their names next to the girl they wanted to take dancing. Zelda was always at the top of the list. It was here to the dismay of chaperones that she danced cheek to cheek and once pinned mistletoe to the seat of her dress.

Civil rights activist Virginia Durr witnessed such a scene: "When she came into a ballroom, all the other girls would want to go home because they knew the boys were going to be concentrating on Zelda. The boys would line up the whole length of the ballroom to dance with her for one minute. She was just preeminent. And we recognized it."

Several photographs show Zelda at the Oak Park

Zelda danced at the Oak Park pavilion.

swimming pool laughing with friends. The pool survived until 1958, when U.S. District Judge Frank M. Johnson Jr. ruled in a civil rights lawsuit that the pool and park must be desegregated. Instead, the city drained the pool, filled it in, and locked the park gates. In February 1965, a fully integrated park was reopened to the public, but the pool and a former small zoo were never restored.

Also of Note

27. Zelda Road

Between Carter Hill Road and Ann Street

Zelda Road is a winding mile and a half business and restaurant hub that dates from the 1960s. Oddly enough, the street was not named for Zelda Fitzgerald but for the road builder's mother, Zelda Franco. That fact seems to have been lost on future builders and developers who quickly cut streets through the area with names such as Gatsby Lane, F. Scott Court, F. Scott Drive, Gatsby Condos, and Zelda Pointe Apartments.

28. Montgomery Museum of Fine Arts

Wynton M. Blount Cultural Park, 1 Museum Drive, Vaughn Road between Eastern Blvd. and Bell Road

The Montgomery Museum of Fine Arts was founded in 1930 by Alabama artist John Kelly Fitzpatrick. It was originally located in a room at Central High School, but in 1959 a modern museum was built on High Street as half of the structure that also housed Montgomery's main public library (and is now solely the Juliette Hampton Morgan Library, named after the Montgomery civil rights martyr). During the 1980s, the city and private individuals collaborated to build a new museum to house its growing collection. Wynton and Carolyn Blount donated thirty-five acres that now includes a state-of-the-art museum, the Alabama Shakespeare Festival, and the Wynton Blunt Cultural Park that includes walking trails, a dog park, and duck ponds. Today, the museum is a small jewel with a superb collection of American paintings, photographs, decorative arts, and sculpture.

Zelda Fitzgerald worked as a visual artist during most of her adult life. She had an exhibition of her paintings in Baltimore in 1932 and in New York City in 1934, and in 1942 she twice exhibited pencil sketches and paintings at the Montgomery Museum of Fine Arts. In 1973, the museum hosted a large, well-received retrospective of her work.

The Museum of Fine Arts owns and occasionally exhibits approximately thirty of Fitzgerald's paintings, including her collection of paper dolls.

I think it would be worthwhile to record your moods while down there. When times are a little calmer I think you ought to have a really inclusive exhibition of your pictures.

— F. SCOTT FITZGERALD,
Dear Scott, Dearest Zelda

29. Taylor Field

Ray Thorington Road

In November 1917, a military airfield was established in Montgomery and named after Captain Robert L. Taylor, who had died in a crash in August 1917. Although primarily a flying school, Taylor Field's eight hundred acres included hangars, repairs shops, and a hospital. One hundred and thirty pilots were stationed here during World War I. Some of these men became Zelda's beaux and performed barrel rolls and other aerial stunts in hopes of impressing her. One mustachioed young suitor was badly injured attempting a tailspin before the field commander banned these dangerous activities. Zelda cut out and pasted the newspaper report of this incident into her scrapbook and then included the incident in *Save Me the Waltz.* The autobiographical heroine, Alabama Beggs, receives news of the incident with a pretense of steely disregard. "We must hold to ourselves and not care."

Taylor Field closed after World War I. It reopened during World War II and then closed permanently in July 1946.

Today, only a plaque near the road commemorates the site. Cattle stand sentinel in a pasture.

30. Camp Sheridan

4 Johnson Avenue, Boylston neighborhood, north of downtown Montgomery

Camp Sheridan is where 1st Lt. Francis Scott Fitzgerald was stationed during World War I. The site was established in 1917 and remained an army camp until the end of the war. It is located in the small community of Boylston, five and a half miles north of downtown Montgomery. The site is marked by three plaques dedicated to several divisions that trained here, including Fitzgerald's own—the 67th Infantry Regiment of the Ninth Division, U.S. Army. From here, Fitzgerald, still unpublished, took taxis or streetcars into town to

*T*he evening and other evenings passed like that, and ended with my going back to camp with the remembered smell of magnolia flowers . . . Taps had been played; there was no sound but the far-away whinny of a horse, and a loud persistent snore at which we laughed, and the leathery snap of a sentry coming to port over by the guardhouse.

— F. Scott Fitzgerald,
   "The Last of the Belles"

attend parties and dances hosted by patriotic citizens and associations to entertain the soldiers. After Zelda's return to Montgomery in the 1940s after Scott's death, she often took long nostalgic walks to the former camp and located the area where Scott's tent once stood.

31. Boodler's Bend

Off Court Street south of town

A lover's lane during the time of World War I, Boodler's was in the southern outskirts of the city past Fleming Road not far from Catoma Creek and today's Hyundai Plant. It was apparently situated in a shaded pecan grove. "Boodling" was youthful slang for necking, and the "Bend" is where many a "petting party" occurred. Zelda and Scott were known to drop by—perhaps after

Afterward they would drive around until they found the center of the summer night and park there while the enchanted silence spread over them like leaves over the babes in the wood.

— F. Scott Fitzgerald, *The Note-Books*

Catoma Creek, south of Montgomery.

a dip in the muddy creek. No doubt they passed around flasks of corn liquor and gin cut with Coke. Today, the area is still rural, with black cows dotting the rolling landscape.

S ay there's one rose that lives and might
   Whisper the fragments of our story:
Kisses, a lazy street—and night.

— F. Scott Fitzgerald,
   "One Southern Girl"

Resources

Bailey, Hugh C., *Edgar Gardner Murphy: Gentle Progressive*, University of Alabama Press, 2003.

Bowsher, Alice Meriwether, and M. Lewis Kennedy Jr., *Alabama Architecture: Looking at Buildings and Place*, University of Alabama Press, 2001.

Bruccoli, Matthew J., Scottie Fitzgerald Smith, and Joan P. Kerr, *The Romantic Egoists*, Charles Scribner's Sons, 1974.

Bruccoli, Matthew J., *Some Sort of Epic Grandeur*, Harcourt Brace Jovanovich, Publishers, 1981.

Bryer, Jackson R., and Cathy W. Barks, editors, *Dear Scott, Dearest Zelda*, St. Martin's Press, 2002.

Cline, Sally, *Zelda Fitzgerald: Her Voice in Paradise*, John Murray Publishers, 2002.

Durr, Virginia Foster, and Hollinger F. Barnard, *Outside the Magic Circle: The Autobiography of Virginia Foster Durr*, University of Alabama Press, 1990.

Fitzgerald, F. Scott, edited by Edmund Wilson, *The Crack-Up*, New Directions, 1945.

Fitzgerald, F. Scott, "The Cruise of the Rolling Junk," *Motor* magazine, 1924.

Fitzgerald, F. Scott, *Flappers and Philosophers,* Charles Scribner's Sons, 1920.

Fitzgerald, F. Scott, "The Ice Palace," *Saturday Evening Post*, 1920.

Fitzgerald, F. Scott, "The Last of the Belles," *Saturday Evening Post*, 1929.

Fitzgerald, F. Scott, "One Southern Girl," 1921 poem, discussed in "Fitzgerald the Poet" by Sena Şen Alta in *Journal of American Studies of Turkey* 45 (2016).

Fitzgerald, F. Scott, *This Side of Paradise*, Charles Scribner's Sons, 1920.

Fitzgerald, F. Scott and Zelda, "Show Mr. and Mrs. F. to Number—," *Esquire*, 1934.

Fitzgerald, Zelda, *Save Me the Waltz*, Charles Scribner's Sons. 1932.

Flynt, Wayne, *Montgomery: An Illustrated History*, Windsor Publications, 1980.

Israel, Suzanne Samuel, *Cloverdale: An Illustrated History*, King Kudzu Publication, 2001.

King, Carole A., and Karren I. Pell, *Montgomery's Historic Neighborhoods*, Arcadia Publishing, 2010.

King, Carole A., and Karren I. Pell, *Montgomery*, Arcadia Publishing, 2011.

Lanahan, Eleanor, *Scottie, The Daughter of. . .*, HarperCollins Publishers, 1995.

Lanahan, Eleanor, *Zelda: An Illustrated Life, the Private World of Zelda Sayre Fitzgerald*, Harry N. Abrams Publishers, 1996.

Landmarks Foundation, Montgomery, Alabama, *Old Oakwood Cemetery: A Brief History*, 2001.

McPhillips, Julian, *Civil Rights in My Bones*, NewSouth Books, 2016.

Milford, Nancy, *Zelda,* Harper and Row Publishers, 1970.

Montgomery Junior League, *A Guide to the City of Montgomery*, Walker Printing Company, 1969.

Neeley, Mary Ann, *Montgomery in the 20th Century*, Landmarks Foundation/HPNbooks, Lammert Incorporated, 2013.

Read, Nicholas Cabell and Dallas, *Deep Family: Four Centuries of American Originals and Southern Eccentrics*, NewSouth Books, 2005.

Stanton, Mary, *Journey toward Justice: Juliette Hampton Morgan and the Montgomery Bus Boycott*, University of Georgia Press, 2006.

Muskat, Beth Taylor, and Mary Ann Neeley, *The Way It Was / 1850–1930 : Photographs of Montgomery and Her Central Alabama Neighbors*, Landmarks Foundation, 1985.

Taylor, Kendall, *Sometimes Madness Is Wisdom*, Ballantine Books, 2001.

Thomson, Bailey, editor, contributor, *A Century of Controversy: Constitutional Reform in Alabama*, University of Alabama Press, 2019.

Thornton, J. Mills, III, and Joseph Caver, *Touched by History: A Self-Guided Tour to Civil Rights Sites in Central Alabama*, the Montgomery Improvement Association by NewSouth Books, 2005.

Trevino, Heather S., and Linda E. Pastorello, *Oak Park and the Montgomery Zoo*, Arcadia Publishing, 2007.

Serafin, Faith, *Haunted Montgomery, Alabama*, the History Press, 2013.

Vaill, Amanda, *Everybody Was So Young: Gerald and Sara Murphy: A Lost Generation Love Story*, Houghton Mifflin Harcourt, 2013.

Wagner-Martin, Linda, *Zelda Sayre Fitzgerald: An American Woman's Life,* Lume Books, 2019.

Acknowledgments

Thanks to: Ken Barr, Wanda Howard Battle, Nathan Brown, Mike Breen, Matthew Byrne, Jane and Arnie Burris, Pat Clark, Lisa Emerson, Lisa Harrison, Gus Katechis, Suzanne La Rosa, John Martello, Leslie and Julian McPhillips, Meredith McDonough, Beth Marino, Dot Moore, Kelly Snyder, Philip Taunton, Randall Williams, and Jannette Wright.

A very special thanks to Alaina Doten, executive director of the F. Scott and Zelda Fitzgerald Museum, for her fine photographs and postcards and engaging and informative discussions about all things Fitzgerald; and to the Alabama Department of Archives and History for facilitating research and providing photos.

Index